SPECIAL PEOPLE
WITH
SPECIAL NEEDS

Written by
Ava Thompson

Illustrations by
Dawn Thompson

AuthorHouse™
1663 Liberty Drive
Bloomington, IN 47403
www.authorhouse.com
Phone: 1 (833) 262-8899

Because of the dynamic nature of the Internet, any web addresses or links contained in this book may have changed since publication and may no longer be valid. The views expressed in this work are solely those of the author and do not necessarily reflect the views of the publisher, and the publisher hereby disclaims any responsibility for them.

Any people depicted in stock imagery provided by Getty Images are models, and such images are being used for illustrative purposes only.
Certain stock imagery © Getty Images.

This book is printed on acid-free paper.

Interior Image Credit: Dawn Thompson

ISBN: 978-1-7283-6921-1 (sc)
978-1-7283-6922-8 (e)

Print information available on the last page.

Published by AuthorHouse 09/25/2020

authorHOUSE®

This Book Is Dedicated To...

The Great Writer and Illustrator of life.

My Father Ken who has shown what tried, tested and true looks like in the flesh.

My Mother, (the late) Celia who pushed through her days with passion and intentional purpose leaving a legacy of resilience to her children.

My "Swift" Uncle Rudolph, the admiration I've had for you as a child only continues to grow.

My (late) Aunty Pris whose love was steadfast, unwavering and unconditional.

My (late) Aunty Hilka who shared her gift of words and writing with the world.

My (late) Sister Shelly Ann who was the 'encourager'.

My Brothers Allingston, Andrew, Bert, Chester, you all are loved beyond measure.

To my large extended family members, old time friends, Greaves kindred, ministry leaders and members, along with my many associates, thank you for your time, prayers, words of inspiration and reassurance, accept this book as my memento of thanks to you.

Honorable Mentor: Lorne, your pure and considerate ways leave footprints of great impression on this earth.

Mentors: Donna, Joan and Marcia words can never express my gratitude for sharing and sowing your knowledge and wisdom.

Special Appreciation to: Angie, Bernice, Gail, Lou, Margo, Sergio, Zainab, and those of you unnamed, thank you for your impact resulting in this significant piece of work.

The Educational, Healthcare, Social Service Organizations, and affiliations with each Director (late) Anne, Manager, Principal, Supervisor, Colleague, Client and Student you gave me the opportunity to learn, grow and share. Know that it is because of your investment in me this notable book has become a reality to empower others!

You the readers, are amazing in your own unique way, share this book with others as a reminder that each person is wonderfully made!

This book should be used as tips for understanding and supporting people with special needs.

It is helpful for individuals, families, educational settings, health care sites, and social service organizations.

Contact:
Agape Support Care Services Inc.
for more information.

People with special needs require extra support in different areas of their lives: at home, school and in the community.

Special needs can include

Neurodevelopmental Disorders such as:

Intellectual Disabilities (ID), Communication Disorders (including language and Speech Disorders), Autism Spectrum Disorder (ASD), Specific Learning Disorders/Disabilities, Motor Disorders and Tic Disorders, Down Syndrome, Williams Syndrome, Prader-Willi Syndrome, etc.

Physical Disabilities such as:

Hearing or Visual Impairment, Cystic Fibrosis (CF), Multiple Sclerosis (MS), Muscular Dystrophy (MD), and Cerebral Palsy (CP), etc.

Setting up a visual lists of things one can do every day, helps people to focus on their tasks. This list can be broken down into bigger or smaller steps for a single task or a whole day, based on the activity itself and the skill level of the individual.

Some people are able to communicate in different ways. For example, one may use pictures to request specific items.

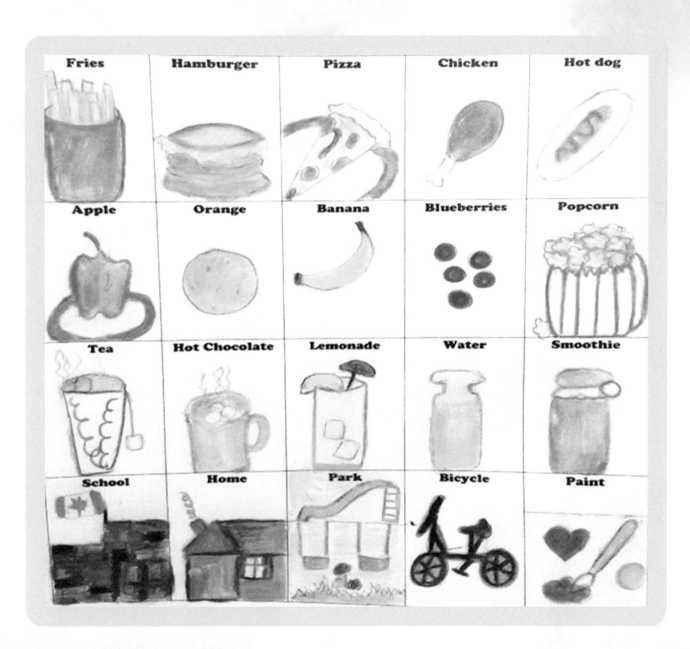

Functional pointing is another way a person can show things they prefer, identify persons they want attention from, the areas or places they desire to go.

Sometimes people yell or scream when they try to communicate feelings of anxiety or anger. Other times, they may react the same when feeling happy or excited. These behaviours can be challenging; as the individual might not have the skills to communicate in appropriate ways.

Looking at the face of a person, noticing their actions, and observing their environment will help you understand what may trigger their reactions. Understanding those triggers can help to prevent future negative outbursts and may assist in maintaining calm behaviour.

Sometimes, when people become overly excited or anxious, they may self-regulate by crying or yelling. Helpful strategies range from using a tension ball to squeeze, physical exercise, music and other sensory methods, which may reduce the anxious behaviour.

The five senses: sight, hearing, smell, taste and touch are primarily used to help a person with special needs understand other people, materials, objects around them, and various aspects of the world. They are often sensitive to certain textures and have a low tolerance for eating particular foods or touching assorted materials.

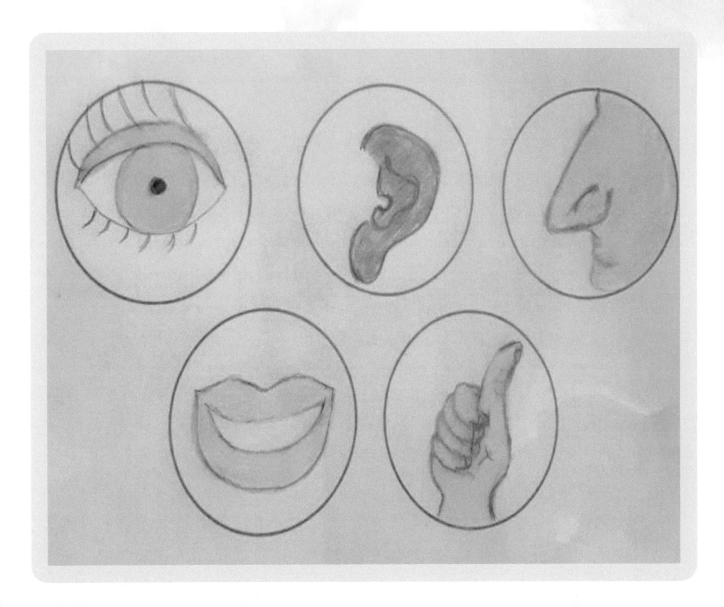

People of support can include parents, caregivers, teachers, medical/clinical staff such as: Family Doctors, Psychologists, members of a behavioural team, Speech and Language Pathologists, along with Occupational Therapists. By observing and assessing a person's behaviour, together with their environmental surroundings, the team can suggest ways to help the person have the best quality of life possible!

The Antecedent, Behaviour, Consequences (ABC) Data Collection Sheet can be used to understand the cause and results of a behaviour, in order for everyone to better help the person.

Skill/Goal Tracking Sheets allow the individual and those supporting them to be aware of their targets to achieve.

A B C
Data Collection Sheet

Name: _____

Date/ Time	Setting	Antecedent (what happen before)	Behaviour (presented behaviour)	Consequences (what happened after)	Notes/Staff

Skill/ Goal Tracking Sheet
Yes - Independent
No- Prompted

Skill/ Goal Language	Date		Date	
	Yes	No	Yes	No
• Read level A book				
•				
•				

Skill/ Goal Mathematics	Date		Date	
	Yes	No	Yes	No
• Add single digits				
•				

Skill/ Goal Life Skill	Date		Date	
	Yes	No	Yes	No
• Tidy up after eating				
•				
•				

There are typically 4 underlying reasons that cause certain behaviours to occur:

1. Sensory – wanting to see, feel, taste, touch or smell something.

2. Escape/Avoidance – wanting to escape or avoid something that is strongly disliked.

3. Attention – wanting to gain the attention or response of others.

4. Tangible – irresistible need to touch or hold something as part of communicating.

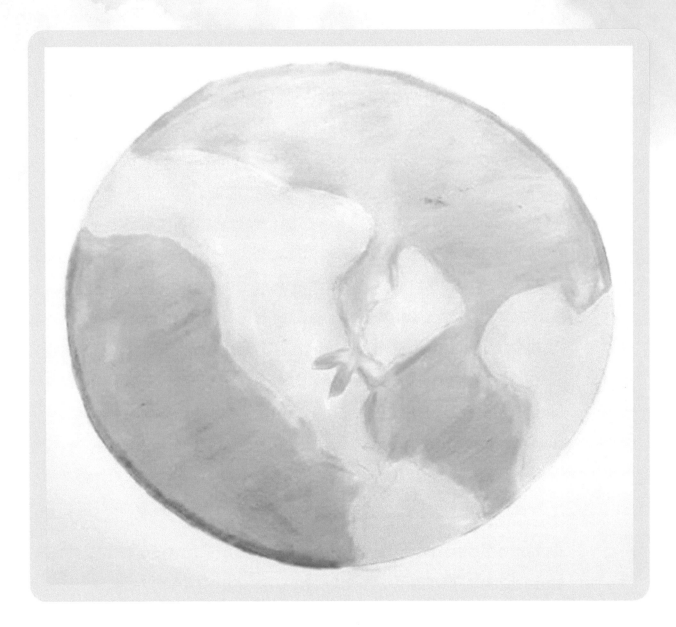

All persons want to be recognized. People with special needs wish to learn about themselves, others, and their world at large which leads to a world of opportunities and possibilities!

DEFINITIONS

The term **"special needs or additional needs"** describes individuals who require assistance because of disabilities that may be medical, mental, physical, or psychological. Guidelines for clinical diagnosis are found in both the Diagnostic Statistical Manual of Mental Disorders (DSM V) and the International Classification of Diseases (ICD 10). Special needs term may be necessary to support individuals with any of these disorders: Autism Spectrum Disorder (ASD), Cerebral Palsy, Down Syndrome, Attention Deficit Hyperactivity Disorder (ADHD), Learning Disability (dyslexia), blindness, deafness, Cystic Fibrosis, Multiple Sclerosis, Muscular Dystrophy, Prader Willi Syndrome.

Autism Spectrum Disorder (ASD) - According to the DSM V, Autism Spectrum Disorder (ASD) is a group of neurodevelopmental disorders where the individual has persistent difficulties with social communication and interaction and restricted, repetitive patterns of behaviour, interests, or activities (Autism Speaks). The characteristics of Asperger syndrome are now included within the broader category of ASD.

Attention Deficit Hyperactivity Disorder - ADHD symptoms fall into two primary categories: (1) inattention and (2) hyperactivity / impulsivity.

Cerebral Palsy - Cerebral Palsy is a group of permanent but non-progressive motor disorders. The onset is usually during early childhood and there might be some milestones delay. Symptoms may include tense and contracted muscles, stiff and jerky movements, poor coordination and balance, and abnormal movements or tremors.

Cystic Fibrosis (CF) – a genetic disorder that affects the lungs and digestive system.

Down Syndrome - 95% of individuals with Down Syndrome have an extra chromosome 21 for a total of three (3) instead of the normal two (2), hence the other term is Trisomy 21. It is usually associated with physical growth delays, mild to moderate intellectual disability, and characteristic facial features. In addition, children may have other medical conditions such as congenital heart defect, digestive problems, and seizures.

Learning Disability - "Learning disabilities refer to a number of disorders which may affect the acquisition, organization, retention, understanding, or use of verbal or nonverbal information. These disorders affect learning in individuals who otherwise demonstrate at least average abilities essential for thinking and/or reasoning." Dyslexia is a learning disorder that involves difficulty reading due to problems identifying speech sounds and learning how they relate to letters and words.

Multiple Sclerosis (MS) - an autoimmune disease of the central nervous system (brain, spinal cord, and optic nerves). Symptoms include extreme fatigue, lack of coordination, weakness, tingling, impaired sensation, vision problems, bladder problems, cognitive impairment, and mood changes.

Muscular Dystrophy - neuromuscular disorder characterized by progressive deterioration of muscle strength. Symptoms include poor balance with frequent falls, muscle weakness, difficulty walking or running, fatigue, and difficulty breathing.

Prader Willi Syndrome (PWS) - rare genetic disorder with the key feature of a constant sense of hunger that usually begins at about 2 years of age and has this constant desire to eat because they never feel full (hyperphagia), and they usually have trouble controlling their weight.

REFERENCES

Autism Speaks. Retrieved from https://www.autismspeaks.ca/about-autism/diagnosis/dsm-5-diagnostic-criteria/

Dyslexia - Mayo Clinic Retrieved from https://www.mayoclinic.org/diseases-conditions/dyslexia/symptoms

ADHD -Theravive - Retrieved from www.theravive.com/therapedia/attention--deficit-hyperactivity-disorder-dsm--5-314.01-(icd-

Learning Disability (LDAC) Retrieved from www.canada.ca/en/public-service-commission/services/public-service-hiring-guide

Multiple Sclerosis - Retrieved from https://mssociety.ca/about-ms

Muscular Dystrophy - Retrieved from https://muscle.ca

Prader Willi Syndrome - Retrieved from https://www.mayoclinic.org/diseases-conditions/prader-willi-syndrome/

Ava Thompson, resides in Toronto, Canada. She is passionate about the lives of people. As a Child and Youth Worker, Teaching Assistant and Consultant with over 25 years experience, she focuses on those with special needs within the educational, health care and social services, from infants to seniors.

An exceptional note of thanks to my sister Dawn for the beautiful illustrations.

Dawn Thompson, lives in Toronto, Canada. She has a plethora of diverse skills complemented to her creative palette such as sketching, poetry, card making and clothing designs. She also enjoys community service work and being the mother of Isaiah who is the light of her life.

To my dear sister Ava, thank you for the opportunity to utilize my gifts and talents in your book. It is a privilege and honour!

Printed in the United States
By Bookmasters